Charles GOUNOD

Messe Solonnelle
"Sainte Cécile"

(Sir Joseph Barnby)

Vocal Score
Klavierauszug

SERENISSIMA MUSIC, INC.

CONTENTS

The final "Domine Salvum" (Prière de l'Église, Prière de l'Armée, Prière de la Nation) at the end of the full score (pp. 127–134) was composed for the specific occaision. It is typically not encountered in performance today and is absent from nearly all vocal scores issued after 1856.

ORCHESTRA

2 Flutes, Piccolo, 2 Oboes, 2 Clarinets, 4 Bassoons
4 Horns, 2 Trumpets, 2 Cornets, 3 Trombones
Timpani, Bass Drum, Cymbals, 6 Harps
Organ
Violin I, Violin II, Viola, Violoncello, Double Bass

Duration: ca. 46 minutes
First performance: November 22, 1855
Paris, Église Saint-Eustache
Soli, Chorus and Orchestra
Conducted by the composer

Complete orchestral parts compatible with this vocal score are available (Cat. No. A2607) from
E. F. Kalmus & Co., Inc.
6403 West Rogers Circle
Boca Raton, FL 33487 USA
(800) 434 - 6340
www.kalmus-music.com

a la mémoire de J. Zimmermann, mon Père

Messe Solonnelle de Ste. Cecile

1. Kyrie

Charles Gounod
Piano reduction by Joseph Barnby

2. Gloria in Excelsis

3. Credo

42

Z260791

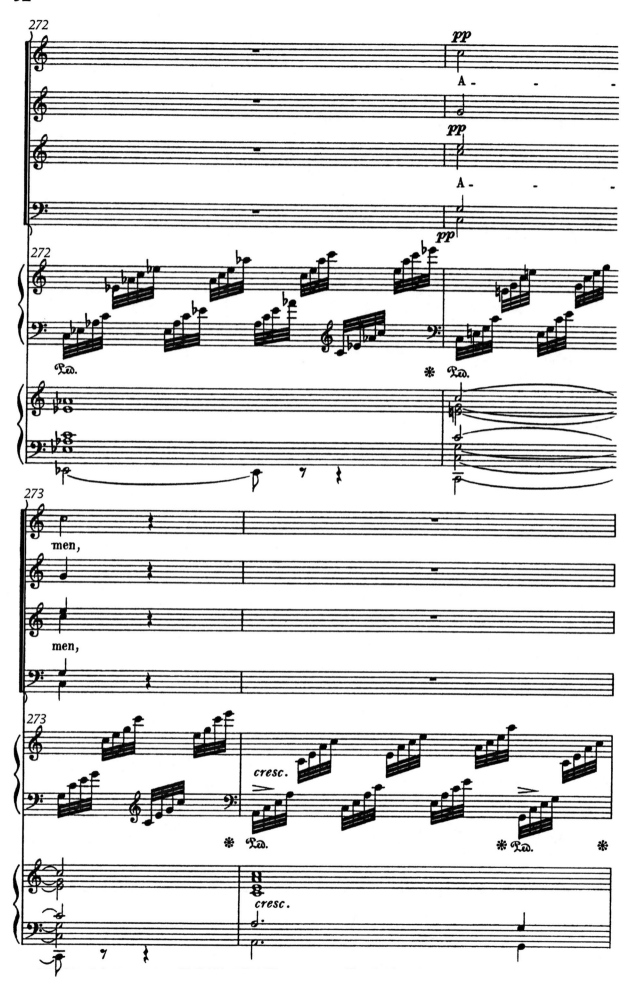

53

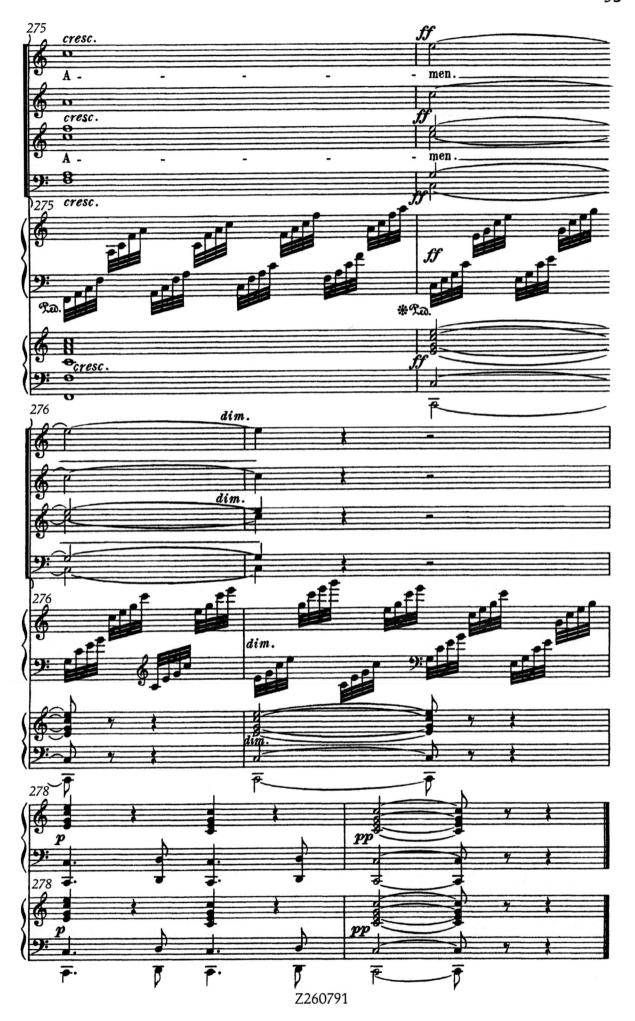

Z260791

3bis Offertoire

(Invocation pour Orchestre Seul)

4. Sanctus

5. Benedictus

6. Agnus Dei

SERENISSIMA MUSIC, INC.

Serenissima publications include digitally-enhanced reprints of authoritative editions for standard classical works, selected titles of lesser-known composers whose music deserves to be made available to a wider audience, and new editions updated to reflect the most recent findings of scholars and performers worldwide.

STUDY SCORES

BACH, Johann Sebastian (1685-1750)
MAGNIFICAT IN D, BWV 243 (NBA, ed. Dürr) SS-640

BEACH, Amy (1868-1944)
SYMPHONY IN E MINOR, Op. 32 "GAELIC" SS-063

CHADWICK, George Whitefield (1854-1931)
SYMPHONY No. 2, Op. 21 .... SS-012
SYMPHONY No. 3 in F SS-020

DEBUSSY, Claude Achille (1862-1918)
CHILDREN'S CORNER (orch. Caplet) SS-055
PETITE SUITE (orch. Büsser) SS-047

MacDOWELL, Edward (1861-1908)
SUITE No. 2, Op. 48 "INDIAN" SS-470

MEDTNER, Nikolai (1880-1951)
PIANO CONCERTO No. 1, Op. 33 .... SS-772

MUSSORGSKY, Modest (1839-1881)
PICTURES AT AN EXHIBITION, FOR WIND ORCHESTRA (orch. Simpson, ed. Reed) SS-101

RIMSKY-KORSAKOV, Nikolai (1844-1908)
SYMPHONY No. 2, Op. 9 "ANTAR" (1897 version) SS-608

SIBELIUS, Jean (1865-1957)
SCENES HISTORIQUES, Opp. 25, 66 .... SS-659

STENHAMMAR, Wilhelm (1871-1927)
SERENADE, Op. 31 .... SS-004

STRAUSS, Johann II (1825-1899)
ROSES FROM THE SOUTH, Op. 388 (ed. McAlister) SS-624
WINE, WOMEN AND SONG, Op. 333 (ed. McAlister) SS-632

SUK, Josef (1874-1935)
FANTASICKE SCHERZO, Op. 25 .... SS-071
POHADKA LETA *(A SUMMER TALE)*, Op. 29 .... SS-594

TCHAIKOVSKY, Peter Ilich (1840-1893)
FRANCESCA DA RIMINI, Op. 32 .... SS-039
SWAN LAKE, BALLET IN FOUR ACTS, Op. 20 (ed. Simpson) SS-616
SWAN LAKE SUITE, Op. 20a (ed. Simpson) SS-314

VOCAL SCORES

BACH, Johann Sebastian (1685-1750)
CANATA No. 4: "CHRIST LAG IN TODES BANDEN", BWV 4 .... Z2493
CANATA No. 31: "DIE HIMMEL LACHT, DIE ERDE JUBILIERET", BWV 31 .... Z5156
CANATA No. 79: "GOTT DER HERR IS SONN UND SCHILD", BWV 79 .... Z2515
CANATA No. 129: "GELOBET SEI DER HERR, MEIN GOTT", BWV 129 .... Z8425
CANATA No. 140: "WACHET AUF, RUFT UNS DIE STIMME", BWV 140 .... Z2530
CANATA No. 150: "NACH DIR, HERR, VERLANGET MICH", BWV 150 (ed. Torvik) Z4521
CANATA No. 191: "GLORIA IN EXCELSIS DEO", BWV 191 (ed. Torvik) Z7520
CHRISTMAS ORATORIO, BWV 248 .... Z2487
MAGNIFICAT IN D, BWV 243 (ed. Straube) Z2488

VOCAL SCORES – CONT.

BEETHOVEN, Ludwig van (1770-1827)
CHORAL FANTASY, OP. 80 (arr. Scharwenka) Z1166
MASS IN C, OP. 86 (arr. Reinecke, ed. Torvik) Z2558
MISSA SOLEMNIS, OP. 123 (arr. Jadassohn) Z2557

BERLIOZ, Hector (1803-1869)
REQUIEM, OP. 5 (arr. Scharwenka) Z2565
TE DEUM, OP. 22 (arr. Barry) Z2568

BRAHMS, Johannes (1833-1897)
GESANG DER PARZEN, OP. 89 (arr. composer) Z2579
NÄNIE, OP. 82 (arr. composer) Z1344
SCHICKSALIED, OP. 54 (arr. composer) Z1343

BRUCKNER, Anton (1824-1896)
MASS IN E MINOR (1882 version) Z2582
PSALM 150 (arr. Hynais, ed. Torvik) Z2583
REQUIEM IN D MINOR (arr. Berberich) Z2584
TE DEUM (1886 version, arr. Schalk) Z2580

CHERUBINI, Maria Luigi (1760-1842)
REQUIEM IN C MINOR (arr. Uhlrich) Z2589
REQUIEM IN D MINOR (arr. Uhlrich) Z2588

DURANTE, Francesco (1684-1755) - mistakenly attr. PERGOLESI
MAGNIFICAT IN B-FLAT (arr. Westermann) Z2703

DVORAK, Antonin (1841-1904)
MASS IN D, OP. 86 (arr. Tours) Z2596
REQUIEM, OP. 89 (arr. composer) Z2595
STABAT MATER, OP. 58 (arr. Zubaty) Z2593
TE DEUM, OP. 103 (arr. Suk, ed. Simpson) Z2594

ELGAR, Edward (1865-1934)
THE MUSIC MAKERS, OP. 69 .... Z0586

FAURE, Gabriel (1845-1924)
REQUIEM, OP. 48 (1900 version, arr. Roger-Ducasse) Z2598

GOUNOD, Charles (1818-1893)
MESSE SOLENNELLE DE STE. CECEILE (arr. Barnby) Z2607
ROMEO ET JULIETTE, CHORUS SCORE (arr. Salomon) Z3029

HANDEL, George Frideric (1685-1759)
CHANDOS ANTHEM IX: "O PRAISE THE LORD WITH ONE CONSENT", HWV 254 (arr. Päsler, ed. Seiffert) ... Z5139
JUDAS MACCABAEUS, HWV 63 .... Z2615

MAHLER, Gustav (1860-1911)
SYMPHONY NO. 8 (arr. Wöss) Z6070

MENDELSSOHN, Felix (1809-1847)
ELIJAH OP. 70 (arr. Kretzschmar) Z2659
ST. PAUL, OP. 36 (arr. Horn, ed. Dörffel) Z2661

MOZART, Wolfgang Amadeus (1756-1791)
BENEDICTUS SIT DEUS, K. 117/66A (arr. Messner) Z2676
MASS IN C MINOR, K. 427 (arr. Schmitt) Z2699
MASS IN C, K. 317 "CORONATION" (arr. Taubmann) Z2694
MISSA BREVIS IN D. K. 194 (arr. Trexler, ed. Torvik) Z2685
REGINA COELI, K. 276 (arr. Scheel) Z2692
REQUIEM, K. 626 (Süssmayr completion, arr. Brissler) Z2670
TE DEUM, K. 141 (arr. Gleichauf, ed. Torvik) Z2678
VENI SANCTE SPIRITUS, K. 47 (arr. Müller) Z2674
VESPERAE SOLENNES DE CONFESSORE, K. 339 (arr. Fuller-Maitland) Z2697

VOCAL SCORES - CONT.

PURCELL, Henry (1659-1695)
DIDO & AENEAS, Z. 626 (arr. Cummings) Z2328

SAINT-SAENS, Camille (1835-1921)
ORATORIO DE NOEL, OP. 12 (arr. Gigout) Z2710

SCHUBERT, Franz Peter (1797-1828)
MASS IN G, D. 167 (arr. Spiro) Z2716
MASS IN E-FLAT, D. 950 (arr. Spengel) Z2718
STABAT MATER, D. 353 (arr. Gohler) Z2720

SCHUMANN, Robert (1810-1856)
REQUIEM, OP. 148 (arr. composer, ed. Torvik) Z7761

VIVALDI, Antonio (1678-1741)
CREDO, RV 591 (arr. Westermann) Z2734
GLORIA, RV 589 (arr. Westermann) Z2732
MAGNIFICAT, RV 610-611 (arr. Westermann) Z2733

CPSIA information can be obtained at www.ICGtesting.com
Printed in the USA
LVOW031846310812

296795LV00001B/20/P